WHAT WAS THE MISSOURI COMPROMISE?

And Other Questions
about the
Struggle over Slavery

Wendy Lanier

LERNER PUBLICATIONS COMPANY · MINNEAPOLIS

A Word about Language

English word usage, spelling, grammar, and punctuation have changed over the centuries. Some spellings in this book have been changed from the original for better understanding.

Lerner Publications Company
A division of Lerner Publishing Group, Inc.
241 First Avenue North
Minneapolis, MN 55401 U.S.A.

Website address: www.lernerbooks.com

Library of Congress Cataloging-in-Publication Data

Lanier, Wendy, 1963–
     What was the Missouri Compromise? : and other questions about the struggle over slavery / by Wendy Lanier.
       p.   cm. — (Six questions of American history)
     Includes bibliographical references and index.
     ISBN 978–0–7613–5331–7 (lib. bdg. : alk. paper)
     1. Missouri compromise—Juvenile literature. 2. Slavery—United States—History—Juvenile literature. 3. United States—Politics and government—1815–1861—Juvenile literature. I. Title.
     E373.L36 2012
     973.5'4—dc23   2011026444

Manufactured in the United States of America
1 – DP – 12/31/11

TABLE OF CONTENTS ... 4

THE SIX
QUESTIONS
HELP YOU
DISCOVER THE
FACTS!

INTRODUCTION

"Order! Gentlemen! Gentlemen, we must have order!" Vice President Daniel D. Tompkins banged his gavel on the desk. Missouri's request for statehood in 1818 had Congress in an uproar. Senators from the North exchanged angry words with those from the South. They were not arguing about money problems or new taxes. The Missouri question was the only thing anyone was talking about.

Members of Congress knew the Missouri question was an important one. The answer would affect the United States for many years. They also knew it would not be easy for them to reach an agreement. Most people had strong feelings one way or another.

The arguing continued for many months. A feeling of uneasiness spread through the halls of Congress. Congressmen on both sides worried that the Union might be dissolved. Kentucky congressman Henry Clay wrote to a friend, "The Missouri subject [controls] all our conversation, all our thoughts. . . . No body seems to think or care about anything else." Speaking to the Senate, Nathaniel Macon of North Carolina said, "The appearance of the Senate

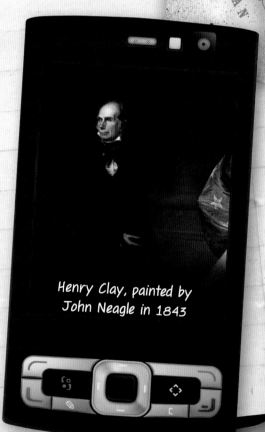

Henry Clay, painted by John Neagle in 1843

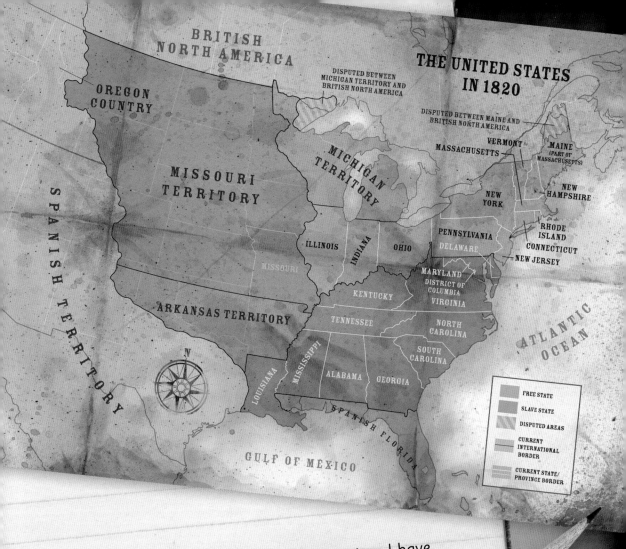

today is different from anything I have seen since I have been a member of it. It is the greatness of the question which has produced it."

Missouri's request for statehood set the stage for a battle that would last more than three years. Why did Missouri's request for statehood cause such an uproar?

In the southern United States, people owned slaves to work in their fields and homes. Slaves pick cotton by hand in this artwork.

ONE THE BIG CONTROVERSY

a form of government where the people have the power to elect representatives

Missouri's request for statehood raised problems that went back to the early days of the republic. Making laws for the new nation was a challenge. The Founding Fathers often disagreed about what the laws should be. Mostly they argued over who should make the laws. Some wanted a strong national government to make laws for all the states. Others believed each state should have the right to make its own laws. One of the biggest arguments was about slavery.

leading figures in the founding of the United States

In 1776 people in all thirteen states owned slaves. In spite of this, many people thought slavery was unjust.

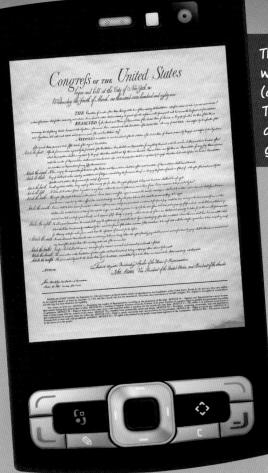

The Bill of Rights is the name that was given to the first ten amendments (additions) to the U.S. Constitution. These amendments help protect certain freedoms and keep the government from being too powerful.

By the late 1780s, the talk of freedom and rights in the U.S. Constitution and the Bill of Rights made people wonder if slavery should be allowed. Soon most northern states took steps to outlaw slavery. Although there were still slaves in the South, most people believed slavery would eventually die out.

But most people in the South depended on agriculture. Workers planted and harvested cash crops like cotton, tobacco, and rice on large farms, called plantations. These crops required lots of hand labor. Plantation owners relied more and more on slaves to do this work.

a crop grown to sell

In 1793 Eli Whitney invented a machine that changed everything. Whitney's cotton gin separated cotton seeds from raw cotton. Suddenly, the job could be done faster and better by machine than by hand. The cotton gin also made it easier to prepare cotton for making cloth. Soon cotton became the main cash crop of the South.

By the early 1800s, many other southern businesses were related to farming. Few large cities existed in the South. Most of the population lived in rural communities. Communities were far apart, and travel was slow and difficult. Fewer people lived in the South than the North.

rural in the country

Eli Whitney invented the cotton gin in 1793.

Eli Whitney

The invention of the cotton gin meant that slaves no longer had to do the tiring work of separating cotton seeds from cotton by hand. More cotton was ready faster for the marketplace, which was good for farmers. Growing cotton became big business in the South in the early 1800s.

HOW WAS CLOTH MADE FROM COTTON BEFORE THE COTTON GIN?

Cotton is a plant that grows in pods on stalks. When the cotton is fully grown, the pods burst open. The raw cotton contains seeds. In the early 1800s, cotton had to be picked by hand. Workers had to remove the seeds by hand too. Sometimes they picked out the seeds. Sometimes they carded the raw cotton. This process involved combing the cotton back and forth between handheld paddles. The paddles were like wire hairbrushes. The carding separated the cotton fibers from the seeds. When the seeds had been removed, the cotton could be spun into yarn or thread. This was done with a spinning wheel or drop spindle. Then the thread was woven into cotton cloth.

In the North, the Industrial Revolution created a different kind of business structure. Years earlier, James Watt had invented the first reliable steam engine. Steam engines could be used to power machinery in factories. Things that used to be made by hand were being made by machines.

the rapid change caused by the introduction of power-driven machines in factories

Francis C. Lowell began using steam-driven machines for spinning and weaving. His large factories in the North were filled with workers making cloth on the new machines. This led to the development of the |textile industry.|

businesses connected with the manufacture of cloth and clothing

Travel was easier in the North too. Robert Fulton used Watt's engine on the first steamboat. Soon, steamboats regularly took passengers as well as products along major rivers in the North. The new National Road, the first paved road, opened a passage west through the Allegheny Mountains.

These new methods and means of transportation allowed people to move quickly and easily. Within a few years, the North was bustling with |commerce.|

the buying and selling of things on a large scale

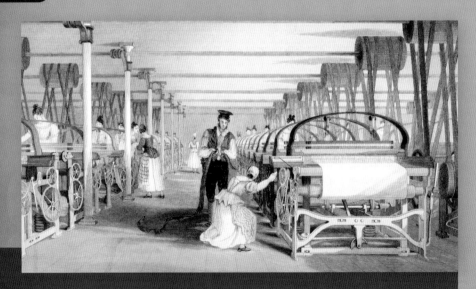

This drawing by Thomas Allom (1804–1872) shows the inside of a textile mill. In northern cities, the textile business boomed. Towns and cities grew up around these factories, which provided jobs to many people. Shops, restaurants, and stores sprang up to meet the needs of factory workers.

The town of Lowell, Massachusetts, located on the Merrimack River, was planned around textile factories.

Factories needed more and more workers to run the new machinery. People moved near the factories to be near their work. Cities grew to have large populations.

Few slaves lived in the North. Less farmwork existed for them there. Most white people did not think slaves could do factory work. White people did not want black people competing with whites for factory jobs. Most people in the North did not welcome African Americans. At the same time, most northerners did not want any new states to allow slavery.

The Missouri Territory was located on what was then the edge of the American frontier. The area was originally part of the Louisiana Purchase. When Louisiana became a state in 1812, all the territory to the north of it was renamed Missouri.

Before the Louisiana Purchase, most of the people living in the Missouri Territory were Native Americans, traders, and fur trappers. After the purchase, settlers began to move in. Many middle-class southern farmers followed. They brought their slaves with them.

LOUISIANA PURCHASE

President Thomas Jefferson purchased 827,987 square miles (2.14 million square kilometers) of land from France in 1803. The land reached from the Mississippi River to the Rocky Mountains and from the Gulf of Mexico to what later became the Canadian border. The Louisiana Purchase doubled the size of the United States. It also provided a free route down the Mississippi River to the Gulf of Mexico and new land for settlers.

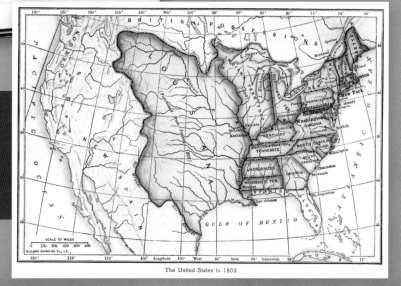

This map shows the area acquired by the United States as a result of the Louisiana Purchase.

The United States in 1803

A French artist living in the United States painted this image of an Osage warrior in 1804. The Osage were native to the Missouri Territory.

Some settlers from the North also went west to the Missouri Territory. They were not used to being around slaves. They did not like southern farmers bringing slaves into the territory. But most of the settlers moving there came from the South. They thought of slaves as personal property. They did not believe anyone had the right to take away their property. They also did not believe anyone could tell them they could not bring slaves into the new territory. Soon most of the settlers in Missouri were slaveholders.

NEXT QUESTION

WHEN DID THE MISSOURI TERRITORY FIRST APPLY FOR STATEHOOD?

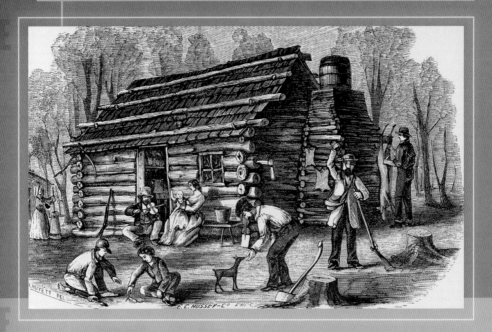

Frontier families, like this one in Missouri, provided for their own needs. They hunted, farmed, and did many other chores. As more people moved to Missouri, they felt ready for statehood.

TWO THE MISSOURI QUESTION

By 1817 the population of the Missouri Territory was more than sixty thousand. The people living there wanted Missouri to become a state. On January 8, 1818, they formally asked Congress to make Missouri the twenty-third state in the Union.

But Missouri's request for statehood presented a problem. Illinois and Alabama were already in line to become states. If the United States added Illinois and Alabama, it would include eleven slave states and eleven free states. All the free states were in the North. The slave states were in the South. Northerners wanted Missouri to be a free state.

HOW DID A TERRITORY BECOME A STATE?

U.S. territories that wanted to become states had to send a request to Congress. A territory became a legal state when Congress approved its request. The request, like any new law, began as a bill. A bill can start in either the House or the Senate. Then members of Congress talk about the bill. Any bill that is approved by both the House and the Senate is sent to the president. The president can sign or veto (reject) it. If the president vetoes a bill, it can still become law. Both the House and the Senate can vote again. If they approve the bill by a two-thirds majority, it becomes a law. But a bill usually becomes a law when the House, the Senate, and the president all agree to it.

Southerners wanted Missouri to be a slave state. Both sides wanted to control Congress.

The Senate that would consider Missouri's request was evenly divided. But in the House of Representatives, there were more northerners than southerners.

The number of representatives a state gets is based on its population. The North's population was larger. This gave them a majority in the House.

The North's advantage in the House was limited by the three-fifths clause, however. The three-fifths clause was a part of the law that allowed the southern states to count every five slaves as three people. This gave the South an extra twenty seats. Although the North controlled the House, it was by a slim majority.

clause, a part of a document or article

Everyone understood that if slavery was allowed in the new territories, the balance of power in Congress would shift. The slave states would gain power. If Congress passed laws to stop the spread of slavery, the power would shift to the free states. Slavery was at the center of a power struggle.

Members of Congress knew the Missouri question did not have an easy answer. They knew months of debate would follow. They were not eager to tackle such a big problem. The congressmen decided to put off the decision until after the election of 1818.

a discussion about the reasons for and against an issue

Samuel F. B. Morse (1791–1872) painted this image of Congress in session. Many sides of the Missouri issue were debated in Congress.

President James Monroe kept an eye on the situation. He was the last of the Founding Fathers to serve as president. He did not believe Congress had the legal power to forbid slavery in new states. He also knew that antislavery ideas were becoming more common. He believed a compromise between proslavery and antislavery groups would be necessary.

the settling of an argument by both sides giving up something

antislavery — opposed to slavery

proslavery — in favor of slavery

"Let us by all wise and constitutional measures promote intelligence among the people as the best means of preserving our liberties."

—President James Monroe, inauguration address, 1817

James Monroe

Pioneers moved westward into territories that were already occupied by Native Americans. Problems arose, and lawmakers had to address issues of transportation, protection, and slavery in new settlements.

Slavery was not the only thing on President Monroe's mind. Settlers moving west into the new territories often had problems with Native Americans. The settlers wanted the government to protect them from attacks. They also wanted better roads to make travel easier.

Protection and good roads came at a price. The only way for the government to pay soldiers, build roads, and make other national improvements was to increase taxes. But many people opposed new taxes.

WHY DID SOUTHERNERS MOVE TO MISSOURI?

Southerners came to Missouri for cheap land. In the South, most of the land belonged to plantation owners. It was hard for middle-class southerners to afford enough land and slave labor to make any money. In Missouri they could afford larger pieces of land. Missouri plantation owners primarily grew hemp, tobacco, and cotton. With slaves to work it, farmers were able to make a profit in a short time.

Native American uprisings, relations with foreign countries, taxes, and slavery were among the main concerns in the election of 1818. The slavery problem alone had the power to shift the balance of power in Congress. It became the most important subject of the election.

Many Missouri farmers grew tobacco. This is an 1860 ad for the Sun Tobacco Works in Saint Louis, Missouri. Saint Louis's location on the Mississippi River meant that goods could easily be shipped to market.

During the election, northerners chose leaders who were strongly opposed to slavery. They wanted the national government to be able to make decisions for all the states. They wanted the government to be able to raise taxes to pay for national improvements.

Southerners chose leaders who were strongly in favor of a state's right to decide the slavery issue. They did not want the national government to have more power than the states. People on both sides of the issue returned to Congress prepared to battle it out.

By November 1818, Congress was back in session. On December 18, 1818, Missouri asked to become a state for the second time. The request went to the floor of the House in February. Congressman James Tallmadge of New York

"It is our business . . . to legislate [pass laws], as never to encourage, but always to control this evil [slavery]. . . ."

—James Tallmadge, in his 1818 speech to the U.S. House of Representatives

James Tallmadge

suggested an amendment to the Missouri bill. He proposed that Missouri be admitted to the United States only if no new slaves were allowed into the state. He also proposed that the children of all current slaves be freed by the age of twenty-five.

Tallmadge's idea sparked an angry debate among the members of the House. Southerners defended the rights of people in Missouri to own slaves. They insisted that slaves were property. No one had the legal right to take a person's property.

SPEECH

OF

THE HONORABLE

JAMES TALLMADGE, Jr.

OF

Duchess County, New-York,

IN THE

House of Representatives of the United States,

ON

SLAVERY.

TO WHICH IS ADDED, THE PROCEEDINGS OF THE

MANUMISSION SOCIETY

OF THE CITY OF NEW-YORK,

AND THE

CORRESPONDENCE OF THEIR COMMITTEE

WITH

Messrs. Tallmadge and Taylor.

NEW-YORK:

PRINTED BY E. CONRAD,

Frankfort-street.

1819.

This is the title page of the printed speech Tallmadge made to the House of Representatives about disallowing more slaves in the new state of Missouri.

The Capitol Building is pictured in 1820, around the time of the debates over the Missouri Compromise. When banks failed and the U.S. economy went bad, Congress had to deal with the financial crisis and put the Missouri issue on hold.

Northerners argued that slavery could not be allowed to expand into the new territories. They said the spread of slavery would hurt the economy of the entire nation. A few argued that slavery was morally wrong. Northern members of the House supported Tallmadge's proposal. Because northern members had a majority in Congress, the amendment was approved.

relating to right and wrong behavior, values, or virtue

Meanwhile, other events were also taking place. In February 1819, the United States faced its first serious money crisis.

The Panic of 1819 caused widespread loss of property. Many banks failed. People lost their jobs. These problems soon caught the attention of Congress. The Missouri question was pushed aside. The Senate never voted on the Tallmadge amendment.

In March 1819, Congress adjourned. The members had made no decision on the Missouri bill. The people of Missouri were still a U.S. territory. Their request for statehood would have to wait.

ended a meeting for a certain amount of time

NEXT QUESTION

WHO WERE THE MEN RESPONSIBLE FOR THE MISSOURI COMPROMISE?

Speaker of the House Henry Clay (standing center) addresses members of Congress. Clay served as Speaker of the House of Representatives from 1811 to 1835.

THREE THE BIG DEBATE

On December 6, 1819, Congress began a new session. The solution to the Missouri question was still undecided. With the help of Jesse B. Thomas of Illinois and Henry Clay, Congress was finally able to reach a compromise.

Henry Clay was the Speaker of the House. Clay believed that the slavery question was a matter for each state to decide. He felt it was not lawful for Congress to make the decision. Clay had become an important political figure, known for his charm, generosity, and forceful speeches. He was a skilled politician and statesman. His work on the Missouri question and other problems earned him the nickname the Great Compromiser.

Speaker of the House: the highest-ranking member of the U.S. House of Representatives

Henry Clay is often considered the author of the Missouri Compromise. But it was Jesse Thomas who first suggested its terms. Thomas was a U.S. senator and a talented lawyer. Although Illinois was a free state, Thomas owned five indentured servants. Thomas usually sided with the southern states on problems discussed in the Senate. But this time, he became one of the first to suggest a solution to the Missouri problem.

people who have agreed to work for someone for a certain amount of time in exchange for travel and living expenses

On December 8, 1819, Congress considered a new item of business. The territory of Maine requested statehood. In the House, Henry Clay saw a chance to help Missouri. He suggested the two applications for statehood be combined. To the northern congressmen, he said, "If you refuse to admit Missouri also free of condition, we see no reason why you shall take to yourselves privileges which you deny to . . . [Missouri]—and, until you grant them also to . . . [Missouri], we will not admit . . . [Maine]."

Henry Clay

HOW DID HENRY CLAY FEEL ABOUT SLAVERY?

Henry Clay believed slavery should be abolished even though he owned slaves. However, he did not believe blacks would ever enjoy the same freedom as whites. He believed the answer to the slavery question was to return freed slaves to Africa. Because of his position, Clay became a founding member of the American Colonization Society (ACS). Its purpose was to return freed slaves to the "homeland." In 1821-1822, the ASC helped found the colony of Liberia for black people who wanted to return to Africa. Clay did not understand that most slaves considered the United States their home.

In the Senate, Jesse Thomas saw the opportunity for compromise. He proposed that Maine and Missouri be admitted to the Union together. One would be a slave state. The other would be free. This would keep the balance of power in the Senate. He also suggested that slavery

These former slaves of Arkansas are awaiting transportation from New York City to Liberia in Africa.

be banned from the Louisiana Purchase north of 36° 30' |latitude,| except for Missouri.

But not everyone was willing to compromise. The debates about the Missouri-Maine bill continued for more than a year. They were often loud and angry. If the compromise passed, it would be the first time Congress had made laws about slavery. (In 1787 members of the Constitutional Convention established the three-fifths law.) The compromise would allow Congress to create laws affecting the entire Union. Many people wondered if Congress had the authority to do this.

Some congressmen argued that the original thirteen states had made their own decisions about slavery. They said that Missouri and Maine should have that right too. They thought Congress could not force Missouri to be a free state.

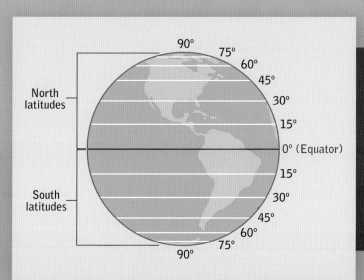

This diagram shows the lines of latitude that circle the globe. The equator in the middle is at 0°. As distance from the equator grows, so do the degrees of latitude. Most of the United States lies between 30° and 45° north latitude.

This image, published with the poem "Our Countrymen in Chains" by John Greenleaf Whittier (1807–1892), reads "Am I not a man and a brother?"

Congress knew that if slavery spread to new states, then slave states would control both the House and the Senate. If slavery was banned from new states, the free states would gain control. The answer to the Missouri question was about more than just statehood. It was about the political future of the entire country.

Jesse Thomas's proposal was finally accepted with some help from Henry Clay. It was not an easy victory. Clay used his position as Speaker to make sure the compromise would pass in the House. To accomplish this, he broke the bill into parts. One part withdrew discussion about outlawing slavery in Missouri. The other part banned slavery north of 36° 30′ latitude except for Missouri. The House voted on each part separately.

Clay told northern congressmen that accepting Missouri as a slave state was the only way to save the Union. At least fourteen of them agreed with him. They voted to support the agreement. Congressman Mark L. Hill of Maine explained his thoughts in a letter to a friend. He said he was "for going as far as any body to restrict Slavery," but only if it could be done "without setting the United States on fire."

In his role as Speaker, Clay appointed only men he knew were open to compromise on the Missouri question to a special committee. When the Missouri-Maine bill was approved, he quickly moved the bill out of the House and back to the Senate. The compromise might never have passed without his influence.

NEXT QUESTION

WHAT WERE THE CONDITIONS OF THE MISSOURI COMPROMISE?

> The committee of conference of the Senate and of the House of Representatives on the subject of the disagreeing votes of the Two Houses, upon the Bill entitled an "Act for the admission of the State of Maine into the Union;" Report the following Resolution.
>
> Resolved.
>
> 1.st That they recommend to the Senate to recede from their amendments to the said Bill
>
> 2.d ... they recommend to ...

FOUR A STATE AT LAST!

The final version of the Missouri Compromise included the following conditions:

1. Maine would be admitted to the Union as a free state.

2. Missouri would be admitted to the Union without limits on slavery.

3. Slavery would be forever banned in all territories of the Louisiana Purchase north of 36° 30' latitude, except in Missouri.

The terms of the Compromise left only the Arkansas and Oklahoma territories open to slavery. It was likely that they would become the next new states. Large numbers

MORE ABOUT THE COMPROMISE

In a compromise, both sides in a dispute get something they want. But each side gives up something too. In the Missouri Compromise of 1820, the northern states allowed Missouri to enter the Union as a slave state. But they succeeded in keeping slavery out of most of the Louisiana Purchase territory. The southern states won an agreement that slavery would continue in Missouri and other southern territories. But they allowed Congress to make decisions about slavery that applied to all states. Both sides got something they wanted even though they had to give up something to get it.

of Americans were already living there. And members of Congress knew that both territories would enter the Union as slave states. The territory north of the 36° 30' was much larger. The Missouri Compromise was a short-term victory for the South. It was a long-term victory for the North.

In March 1820, Maine was admitted to the Union. Congress authorized Missouri to write a set of laws for its state government. Missouri could not actually become a state until those laws were approved by Congress.

As part of the Missouri Compromise, Maine was admitted into the Union. This letter, dated March 3, 1820, announces Maine's new statehood, which would become official on March 15.

31

The people of Missouri were already angry over the slavery debate. They did not believe Congress should interfere in what they considered a local matter. Nevertheless, during the summer of 1820, Missouri held a convention to create its new state laws. Missourians elected mostly proslavery delegates to the convention. The laws they wrote included certain parts that antislavery northerners did not like.

representatives to a convention

For example, free blacks or anyone of mixed race could not enter Missouri. It was not the only state to have this condition. But the condition was not legal. The U.S. Constitution clearly states that "the citizens of each State shall be entitled to all [the] privileges . . . of citizens in the several States." This meant that free blacks living in any state had the right to move from state to state without risking their freedom.

Another Missouri law banned the state from freeing slaves without the owner's permission. Northern congressmen urged Congress not to approve the new laws. They accused Missouri of treating citizens of other states unfairly.

The new laws set the stage for another battle in Congress. Missouri's quest for statehood was once again the main topic of Congress. During the months of angry debate, many delegates feared the Union would not survive.

"The citizens of each state shall be entitled to all [the] privileges . . . of citizens in the several states."

—U.S. Constitution

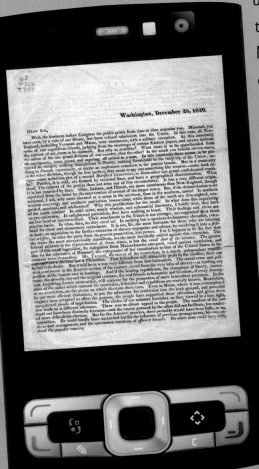

U.S. Representative Joshua Cushman of Massachusetts wrote this letter, dated December 25, 1820, supporting Congress's decision to vote against the Missouri Compromise.

The House rejected Missouri's state laws by a vote of 93 to 79. Francis Jones of Tennessee was dismayed by the vote. "I am sorry to tell you," he wrote to a friend, "that in my opinion, in fact the Union is now almost dissolved. I declare to you, that when the result of the vote was announced, my feelings were inexpressible."

The situation seemed hopeless. Then Henry Clay suggested another compromise. Clay had been away from Washington, D.C., on personal business. Someone else was serving as Speaker of the House. Clay returned to Congress in January 1821. He quickly became the driving force behind a second Missouri Compromise.

This photograph of Henry Clay and his wife, Lucretia, was taken in 1849 on their fiftieth wedding anniversary. Clay was instrumental in writing and pushing through the Missouri Compromise.

Clay proposed that Missourians rewrite the laws. They would leave out the part that made it unlawful for free blacks to enter Missouri. They would write a new part stating that Missouri would not treat citizens from other states unfairly.

First, Congress had to agree to Clay's proposal. The new bill passed the House by a vote of 87 to 81. Two days later, on February 28, 1821, the Senate passed the second Missouri Compromise. The vote was 28 to 14. In June Missouri lawmakers grudgingly agreed to make the changes.

Finally, on August 10, 1821, President James Monroe signed the bill admitting Missouri to the Union as the twenty-fourth state. The long wait was over. It had been more than three years since Missouri first asked to enter the Union.

NEXT QUESTION

WHERE WAS THE MISSOURI COMPROMISE MET WITH THE STRONGEST RESPONSE?

The U.S. Capitol Building in Washington, D.C., is where the House and Senate meet to debate and vote on matters of the country. Arist John Rubens Smith (1775-1849) made this painting.

FIVE THE COUNTRY'S RESPONSE

The Missouri agreement ended the debates in Congress for a time. But it was just the beginning of the public debate about the decision. Americans, especially those in the North, questioned whether a nation where "all men are created equal" should allow slavery to continue.

Before the Missouri Compromise, most Americans gave little thought to slavery. A small part of the population was morally opposed to slavery. These people believed it was not right. Most people, however, had been more concerned by the country's economic depression.

a time when business is bad and many people lose their jobs

The Missouri question brought the slavery problem to the public's attention again.

In 1820 most politicians saw the slavery debate as part of a power struggle for control of Congress. They did not think of slavery as being wrong. No congressmen said slavery should be stopped in states where it already existed. For most lawmakers, the question of slavery was political.

The solution to the Missouri problem brought a temporary cease-fire to Congress. But most members knew the question would come up again. The Missouri agreement held for thirty years.

A wagon train crosses the prairie. As new states were formed, the issue of slavery would continue to arise.

NOTICE.

THE DUTCHESS COUNTY ANTI-SLAVERY SOCIETY

Will hold its first Annual Meeting at the house of Stephen E. Flagler, in the village of *Pleasant Valley,*

ON THURSDAY,

The 25th inst.

☞ Several gentlemen will **ADDRESS** the meeting.☜

A neat and spacious Room, fitted for a large audit of Ladies and Gentlemen, is provided for the occasion.

All who feel an interest in the PRESE VATION OF THEIR LIBERTIES are respect-fully invited to attend.

P. S. Meeting for Business at 11, A. M.—for Ad dresses at half past 2, P. M.

April 22, 1839.

During those years, opposition to slavery began to grow in the North. While Congress was still debating the Missouri Compromise, antislavery supporters were already hard at work. They organized meetings, wrote letters to newspapers, and sent hundreds of pamphlets. These activities raised awareness in the North. Groups formed to end slavery. The antislavery movement gained many supporters during this time.

short, printed booklets

Most southerners continued to defend slavery. They needed slaves to work the farms. Banning slavery would risk their way of living. They were angry that Congress had focused the nation's attention on slavery. Southerners strongly believed slavery was a matter for local and state governments to decide.

Meanwhile, the people of Missouri were happy the long battle for statehood had finally ended. Missourians were anxious to get back to making a life on the frontier. It took hard work to survive in the wilderness. Everyone had to work. The farmers, their slaves, and even children had to do their part.

Sometimes families made a party of their work. These gatherings were called bees. Music and dancing began when the work was done. The children played games while the adults danced. The bees were a welcome change from the usual farm life.

This painting by U.S. artist John Lewis Krimmel from 1813, titled *Quilting Party*, shows how people came together for work and fun to make light of chores. The stylized portrayal of slaves in this image was typical of early American art.

Although Missourians wanted to forget about their battle for statehood, the conflict over the Missouri question threatened the stability of the United States. Some of the patriots who had fought to win America's freedom were still alive. They were alarmed by the talk of dissolving the Union. Among these patriots was Thomas Jefferson.

Jefferson had put his own life in danger to help gain the freedom of the new nation. He was a Founding Father and the author of the Declaration of Independence.

WHEN DID THE MISSOURI COMPROMISE END?

In 1854 the Kansas-Nebraska Act replaced the 36° 30' line established by the Missouri Compromise of 1820. The bill provided for "popular sovereignty" in Kansas and Nebraska. That meant that the settlers in those territories—rather than Congress—would decide all slavery questions. The Missouri Compromise was declared "inoperative and void." The Kansas-Nebraska Act made slavery legally possible in new territories north of the 36° 30' line.

Thomas Jefferson

THE DRED SCOTT CASE

In 1857 the Dred Scott case came before the U.S. Supreme Court, the highest court. Scott (right) was a slave who sued for his freedom because, at times, he had lived in places where slavery was forbidden. The Supreme Court ruled that Scott could not sue because slaves were not citizens. Only citizens had the right to sue. The Court also ruled that slaves were property. The court said Congress could not forbid slavery in the territories without violating a slave owner's constitutional right to own property. The Supreme Court's decision angered antislavery supporters. The Kansas-Nebraska Act and the outcome of the Dred Scott case were contributing factors to the outbreak of the Civil War in 1861.

By 1820 The Jefferson had already served terms as presic and oversaw the Louisiana Purchase. Jeffe realized that the questions about slavery and states' rights were dividing the country and putting the Ur at risk.

NEXT QUESTION

HOW DO WE KNOW THOMAS JEFFERSON WAS WORRIED ABOUT THE UNION DISSOLVING?

Primary Source: Thomas Jefferson's Letter to John Holmes

The best way to see into the past and learn about events in history is with primary sources. A primary source is a document written by someone alive at the time an event took place. Letters, journals, diaries, newspaper articles, and government papers are examples of primary sources. In the primary source below, Jefferson discusses his concerns about the Union dissolving. He is writing a letter to John Holmes, a congressman from Maine. Holmes had supported the Missouri Compromise. He defended his vote in a letter to the people of Maine. He sent a copy of the letter to Thomas Jefferson. In response Jefferson wrote:

> I thank you, Dear Sir, for the copy you have been so kind to send me of the letter to your constituents [a voter represented by an elected official] on the Missouri question. . . . [T]his . . . question, like a fire bell in the night, awakened and filled me with terror. I considered it at once as the knell [death announcement] of the Union. It is hushed indeed for the moment, but this is a reprieve only, not a final sentence.
>
> As it is, we have the wolf by the ear, and we can neither hold him, nor safely let him go. . . . I regret that I am now to die in the belief that the useless sacrifice of themselves, by the generation of [1776] to acquire self government . . . is to be thrown away . . . and that my only consolation is to be that I live not to weep over it.

TELL YOUR MISSOURI COMPROMISE STORY

You are a senator from a northern or southern state in 1820.

WHO are you?

WHERE is your home?

HOW did you travel to Washington?

WHAT issues are most important to you?

HOW will you vote on the Missouri Compromise?

WHY will you vote this way?

USE **WHO, WHAT, WHERE WHY, WHEN,** AND **HOW** TO THINK OF OTHER QUESTIONS TO HELP YOU CREATE YOUR STORY!

Timeline

1818

On January 8, Missouri requests admission to the Union as a slave state. Congress ends its session without considering the request.

On December 18, Missouri requests to be admitted to the Union again.

1819

Missouri's request for statehood—called the Missouri bill—is talked about in the House on February 13.

On February 17, James Tallmadge of New York proposes an amendment to the Missouri bill. It says no new slaves will be admitted to the state and children of current slaves will be freed. The amendment passes in the House, but the Senate never votes on it.

On March 4, Congress stops working without a decision on the Missouri bill.

On August 30, a meeting is held by a group that wants to forbid slavery in Missouri.

Congress begins a new session on December 6.

Maine applies for statehood as a free state on December 8.

On December 30, **Henry Clay** declares that if Missouri is not admitted to the Union without limits on slavery, then Maine will not be admitted either.

1820

A bill from the House suggesting that requests for statehood by Missouri and Maine be combined moves to the Senate on January 13.

Senator Jesse B. Thomas suggests that slavery be forever outlawed north of 36° 30′ latitude except within the boundaries of Missouri. This becomes the basis for the Missouri Compromise.

The Senate agrees to combine the Missouri and Maine bills on February 16.

On February 18, the Senate passes a joint Missouri-Maine bill including the Thomas amendment. The bill is returned to the House.

The House rejects the Senate version of the Missouri-Maine bill on February 23. A joint meeting between members of the House and Senate is called.

On March 2, the House votes that Missouri be allowed to enter the Union without limits on slavery and that slavery be forever banned in all territories north of 36° 30'. This does not include the state of Missouri.

Congress passes the Missouri Compromise on March 3.

On March 6, Congress authorizes Missouri to write state laws and create a state government without limits on slavery.

Maine is admitted to the Union as the twenty-third state on March 15.

The new Missouri legislature adopts Missouri's first state laws on July 19.

Missouri's first state elections are held on August 28.

1821

Congress rejects Missouri's state laws in February.

Congress passes a second Missouri Compromise on February 28.

In June Missouri agrees to change the wording of its state laws to show that no laws will be passed that might interfere with the rights of U.S. citizens.

Missouri is admitted to the Union as the twenty-fourth state on August 10.

1854

The Kansas-Nebraska Act replaces the line established by the Missouri Compromise of 1820. New states added to the Union can decide the slavery question for themselves.

1857

U.S. Supreme Court tries the Dred Scott Case.

Source Notes

4 Henry Clay to John J. Crittenden, January 29, 1820, in *The Life of John J. Crittenden, with Selections from His Correspondence and Speeches*, ed. Mrs. Chapman Coleman (Philadelphia: J. B. Lippincott & Co., 1893), 40.

4–5 *Annals of Congress*, Senate, 16th Cong., 1st sess., 97.

17 Tallmadge, James, *Speech of the Honorable James Tallmadge, Jr. of Duchess County, New York on Slavery*, 1819, available online at Internet Archive, http://www.archive.org/details/speechofhonorabl00tall (November 14, 2011).

20 James Monroe, First Inaugural Address, March 4, 1817, available online at Bartleby.com, 2011, http://www.bartleby.com/124/pres20.html (November 16, 2011).

25 *Annals of Congress*, House of Representatives, 16th Cong., 1st sess., 841–842.

29 Mark L. Hill to William King, January 28, 1820, in Glover Moore, *The Missouri Controversy 1819–1821* (Lexington: University of Kentucky Press, 1953), 105.

32–33 U.S. Constitution, art. 4, sect. 2.

34 Francis Jones, January 2, 1821 in Glover Moore, *The Missouri Controversy 1819–1821*, (Lexington, Kentucky: University of Kentucky Press, 1953), 151.

42 Thomas Jefferson to John Holmes, April 22, 1820, Thomas Jefferson Papers, Library of Congress, August 3, 1010, http://www.loc.gov/exhibits/jefferson/159.html (November 16, 2011).

Selected Bibliography

Clay, Henry. *The Papers of Henry Clay 1777–1852*. Lexington: University of Kentucky Press, 1992.

Forbes, Robert Pierce. *The Missouri Compromise and Its Aftermath*. Chapel Hill: University of North Carolina Press, 2007.

Jefferson, Thomas. *The Thomas Jefferson Papers 1601–1827*. Library of Congress, American Memory. N.d. http://memory.loc.gov/ammem/collections/jefferson_papers/ (November 16, 2011).

Mason, Matthew. *Slavery and Politics in the Early American Republic*. Chapel Hill: University of North Carolina Press, 2006.

Moore, Glover. *The Missouri Controversy 1819–1821*. Lexington: University of Kentucky Press, 1953.

Further Reading and Websites

Donovan, Sandy, and Robin Nelson. *The Congress*. Minneapolis: Searchlight Books, 2012. Learn all about the U.S. Congress with this engaging title. It's packed with interesting photos and informative text. You'll discover how Congress passes laws and how it relates to the other branches of government.

Dudley, Susan. *Missouri Compromise. Landmark Legislation*. New York: Benchmark Books, 2010. For older kids, this is a young adult book about the Missouri Compromise.

Fact Monster—Missouri Compromise
http://www.factmonster.com/ce6/history/A0833427.html
Go to this site for fun facts.

LaDoux, Rita C. *Missouri*. Minneapolis: Lerner Publications Company, 2002.

Missouri Compromise for Kids
http://www.socialstudiesforkids.com/wwww/us/missouricompromisedef.htm
This website for kids offers information on various social studies topics, including the Missouri Compromise.

Missouri Kids! Office of the Secretary of State
http://www.sos.mo.gov/kids/
Learn all about the state of Missouri including its history and famous people.

Ransom, Candice. *Who Wrote the U.S. Constitution? And Other Questions about the Constitutional Convention of 1787*. Minneapolis: Lerner Publications Company, 2011. Discover how our Founding Fathers managed to produce this incredible document. The Constitution represents a turning point in American history, and it remains the basis of our legal system.

Sherrow, Victoria. *Thomas Jefferson*. Minneapolis: Lerner Publications Company, 2002. Read this short biography of Thomas Jefferson to find out more about his life.

Thomas Jefferson: Library of Congress Exhibit
http://www.loc.gov/exhibits/jefferson/159.html
Visit this site to read Thomas Jefferson's entire letter to John Holmes.

Index

Photo Acknowledgments

The images in this book are used with the permission of: © iStockphoto.com/DNY59, p. 1; © Picsfive/Shutterstock.com, p. 1 and all chain backgrounds; © iStockphoto.com/sx70, pp. 3 (top), 9 (bottom), 12 (top), 15, 19 (top), 26 (top), 31 (top), 40 (right), 41 (left); © iStockphoto.com/Ayse Nazli Deliormanli, pp. 3 (bottom), 43 (bottom); © iStockphoto.com/Serdar Yagci, pp. 4-5, (background), 43 (background); © Bettmann/CORBIS, pp. 4 (inset), 25, 44; © iStockphoto.com/Andrey Pustovoy (smart phone), pp. 4, 7, 8, 33, 38; © Laura Westlund/Independent Picture Service (maps), pp. 4-5, 27, 32; © Hulton Archive/Stringer/Getty Images, p. 6; © Aaron Haupt/Photo Researchers/Getty Images, p. 7 (inset); © SuperStock, p. 8 (left); © Fritz Goro/Time & Life Pictures/Getty Images, p. 8 (right inset); © Private Collection/Peter Newark American Pictures/The Bridgeman Art Library International, p. 9 (top); © Universal History Archive/Hulton Archive/Getty Images, p. 10; The Granger Collection, New York, pp. 11, 13 (top), 16, 19 (bottom), 21, 39; © North Wind Picture Archives/Alamy, p. 12 (bottom); © CORBIS, p. 14; © Stock Montage/Getty Images, p. 17; © Rischgitz/Hulton Archive/Getty Images, p. 18; Print Collection, Miriam and Ira D. Wallach Division of Art, Prints and Photographs, The New York Public Library, Astor, Lenox and Tilden Foundations, p. 20; © MPI/Stringer/Getty Images, pp. 22, 24, 36; Schomburg Center for Research in Black Culture/Photographs and Prints Division, The New York Public Library, Astor, Lenox and Tilden Foundations, p. 26 (bottom); Library of Congress (LC-USZC4-5321), p. 28; Our Documents/National Archives, p. 30; Collections of Maine Historical Society, pp. 31 (bottom), 33 (inset), 45; Courtesy of Ashland, The Henry Clay Estate, Lexington, Kentucky, p. 34; © Fotosearch/Stringer/Getty Images, p. 37; Manuscripts and Archives Division, The New York Public Library, Astor, Lenox and Tilden Foundations, p. 38 (inset); © Herbert Orth/Time & Life Pictures/Getty Images, p. 40 (left); Missouri History Museum, St. Louis, p. 41 (right); © Everett Collection/SuperStock, p. 43 (map).

Front cover: © Laura Westlund/Independent Picture Service. Back cover background: © Picsfive/Shutterstock.com.

Main body text set in Sassoon Sans Regular 13.5/20. Typeface provided by Monotype Typography.